PERFORMANCE
EDITIONS

BEETHOVEN

PIANO SONATA NO. 32
IN C MINOR
Opus 111

Edited and Recorded by Robert Taub

Also Available:
BEETHOVEN PIANO SONATAS
edited and recorded by Robert Taub

Volume I, Nos. 1–15
00296632 Book only
00296634 CDs only (5 disc set)

Volume II, Nos. 16–32
00296633 Book only
00296635 CDs only (5 disc set)

On the cover:
The Tree of Crows, 1822 (oil on canvas)
by Caspar David Friedrich
(1774–1840)

ISBN 978-1-4768-1641-8

G. SCHIRMER, *Inc.*

Distributed By

HAL•LEONARD® CORPORATION
7777 W. Bluemound Rd. P.O. Box 13819 Milwaukee, WI 53213

CONTENTS

PAGE	TRACK	
4		BEETHOVEN AND THE PIANO SONATAS
6		PERFORMANCE NOTES
		Piano Sonata No. 32 in C minor, Opus 111
9	1	Maestoso; Allegro con brio ed appassionato
19	2	Arietta: Adagio molto semplice e cantabile
35		ABOUT THE EDITOR

BEETHOVEN
AND THE PIANO SONATAS

In 1816, Beethoven wrote to his friend and admirer Carl Czerny: "You must forgive a composer who would rather hear his work just as he had written it, however beautifully you played it otherwise." Having lost patience with Czerny's excessive interpolations in the piano part of a performance of Beethoven's *Quintet for Piano and Winds*, Op. 16, Beethoven also addressed the envelope sarcastically to "Herr von Zerni, celebrated virtuoso." On all levels, Beethoven meant what he wrote.

As a composer who bridged the gulf between court and private patronage on one hand (the world of Bach, Handel, Haydn, and Mozart) and on the other hand earning a living based substantially on sales of printed works and/or public performances (the world of Brahms), Beethoven was one of the first composers to become almost obsessively concerned with the accuracy of his published scores. He often bemoaned the seeming unending streams of mistakes. "Fehler—fehler!—Sie sind selbst ein einziger Fehler" ("Mistakes—mistakes!—You yourselves are a unique mistake") he wrote to the august publishing firm of Breitkopf und Härtel in 1811.

It is not surprising, therefore, that toward the end of his life Beethoven twice (1822 and again in 1825) begged his publishers C.F. Peters and Schott to bring out a comprehensive complete edition of his works over which Beethoven himself would have editorial control, and would thus be able to ensure accuracy in all dimensions—notes, pedaling and fingering, expressive notations (dynamics, slurs), and articulations, and even movement headings. This never happened.

Beethoven was also obsessive about his musical sketches that he kept with him throughout his mature life. Desk sketchbooks, pocket sketchbooks: thousands of pages reveal his innermost compositional musings, his labored processes of creativity, the ideas that he abandoned, and the many others—often jumbled together—that he crafted through dint of extraordinary determination, single-minded purpose, and the inspiration of genius into works that endure all exigencies of time and place. In the autograph scores that Beethoven then sent on to publishers, further layers of the creative processes abound. But even these scores might not be the final word in a particular work; there are instances in which Beethoven made textual changes, additions, or deletions by way of letters to publishers, corrections to proofs, and/or post-publication changes to first editions.

We can appreciate the unique qualities of the Beethoven piano sonatas on many different levels. Beethoven's own relationship with these works was fundamentally different from his relationship to his works of other genres. The early sonatas served as vehicles for the young Beethoven as both composer and pianist forging his path in Vienna, the musical capital of Europe at that time. Throughout his compositional lifetime, even when he no longer performed publicly as a pianist, Beethoven used his thirty-two piano sonatas as crucibles for all manner of musical ideas, many of which he later re-crafted—often in a distilled or more rarefied manner—in the sixteen string quartets and the nine symphonies.

The pianoforte was evolving at an enormous rate during the last years of the eighteenth century extending through the first several decades of the nineteenth. As a leading pianist and musical figure of his day, Beethoven was in the vanguard of this technological development. He was not content to confine his often explosive playing to the smaller sonorous capabilities of the instruments he had on hand; similarly, his compositions demanded more from the pianofortes of the day—greater depth of sonority, more subtle levels of keyboard finesse and control, and increased registral range.

These sonatas themselves pushed forward further development and technical innovation from the piano manufacturers.

Motivating many of the sonatas are elements of extraordinary—even revolutionary—musical experimentation extending into domains of form, harmonic development, use of the instrument, and demands placed upon the performer, the piano, and the audience. However, the evolution of these works is not a simple straight line.

I believe that the usual chronological groupings of "early," "middle," and "late" are too superficial for Beethoven's piano sonatas. Since he composed more piano sonatas than substantial works of any other single genre (except songs) and the period of composition of the piano sonatas extends virtually throughout Beethoven's entire creative life, I prefer chronological groupings derived from more specific biographical and stylistic considerations. I delve into greater depth on this and other aspects of the sonatas in my book *Playing the Beethoven Piano Sonatas* (Amadeus Press).

1795–1800: Sonatas Op. 2 no. 1, Op. 2 no. 2, Op. 2 no. 3, Op. 7, Op. 10 no. 1, Op. 10 no. 2, Op. 10 no. 3, Op. 13, Op. 14 no. 1, Op. 14 no. 2, Op. 22, Op. 49 no. 1, Op. 49 no. 2

1800–1802: Sonatas Op. 26, Op. 27 no. 1, Op. 27 no. 2, Op. 28, Op. 31 no. 1, Op. 31 no. 2, Op. 31 no. 3

1804: Sonatas Op. 53, Op. 54, Op. 57

1809: Sonatas Op. 78, Op. 79, Op. 81a

1816–1822: Sonatas Op. 90, Op. 101, Op. 106, Op. 109, Op. 110, Op. 111

From 1804 (post-Heiligenstadt) forward, there were no more multiple sonata opus numbers; each work was assigned its own opus. Beethoven no longer played in public, and his relationship with the sonatas changed subtly.

—Robert Taub

PERFORMANCE NOTES

Extracted from *Beethoven: Piano Sonatas Volume II*, edited by Robert Taub.

For the preparation of this edition, I have consulted autograph scores, first editions, and sketchbooks whenever possible. (Complete autograph scores of only twelve of the piano sonatas—plus the autograph of only the first movement of Sonata Op. 81a—have survived.) I have also read Beethoven's letters with particular attention to his many remarks concerning performances of his day and the lists of specific changes/corrections that he sent to publishers. We all know—as did Beethoven—that musical notation is imperfect, but it is the closest representation we have to the artistic ideal of a composer. We strive to represent that ideal as thoroughly and accurately as possible.

Tempo

My recordings of these sonatas are available as companions to the two published volumes. I have also included my suggestions for tempo (metronome markings) for each sonata, at the beginning of each movement.

Fingering

I have included Beethoven's own fingering suggestions. His fingerings—intended not only for himself (in earlier sonatas) but primarily for successive generations of pianists—often reveal intensely musical intentions in their shaping of musical contour and molding of the hands to create specific musical textures. I have added my own fingering suggestions, all of which are aimed at creating meaningful musical constructs. As a general guide, I believe in minimizing hand motions as much as possible, and therefore many of my fingering suggestions are based on the pianist's hands proceeding in a straight line as long as musically viable and physically practicable. I also believe that the pianist can develop senses of tactile feeling for specific musical patterns.

Pedaling

I have also included Beethoven's pedal markings in this edition. These indications are integral parts of the musical fabric. However, since most often no pedal indication is offered, whenever necessary one should use the right pedal—sparingly and subtly—to help achieve legato playing as well as to enhance sonorities.

Ornamentation

My suggestions regarding ornamental turns concern the notion of keeping the contour smooth while providing an expressive musical gesture with an increased sense of forward direction. The actual starting note of a turn depends on the specific context: if it is preceded by the same note (as in Sonata Op. 10 no. 2, second movement, m. 42), then I would suggest that the turn is four notes, starting on the upper neighbor: upper neighbor, main note, lower neighbor, main note.

Sonata in F Major, Opus 10 no. 2:
second movement, m. 42, r.h.

However, if the turn is preceded by another note (as in Sonata Op. 10 no. 2, first movement, m. 38), then the turn could be five notes in total, starting on the main note: main note, upper neighbor, main note, lower neighbor, main note.

Sonata in F Major, Opus 10 no. 2:
first movement, m. 38, r.h.

Whenever Beethoven included an afterbeat (Nachschlag) for a trill, I have included it as well. When he did not, I have not added any.

Footnotes

Footnotes within the musical score offer contextual explanations and alternatives based on earlier representations of the music (first editions, autograph scores) that Beethoven had seen and corrected. In areas where specific markings are visible only in the autograph score, I explain the reasons and context for my choices of musical representation. Other footnotes are intended to clarify ways of playing specific ornaments.

Notes on the Sonata[1]

PIANO SONATA NO. 32 IN C MINOR, OPUS 111 (1822)

Sonata Op. 111 is an enormous expressive challenge to pianists, to pianos, and to listeners, for no matter how many times we have played or heard this work, there are new aural connections to be made, deeper realms of emotional involvement, new perceptions to be felt.

The drama is riveting from the start. I sit up straight, and when I have heard the tempo of the opening measures internally and established the maestoso feeling of the opening to the **Maestoso**, I place my left hand on the first E-flat octave. I then look at the second octave that the left hand plays—the F-sharp octave—hearing once again the tension inherent in this diminished seventh interval, and only then do I play the first two chords, using the thumb as a guide to make sure that there are no extraneous notes. While the F-sharp octave is reverberating, I place my right hand on its first chord and complete the first two-measure phrase, insuring that the trill receives special dynamic emphasis and that the chords in m. 2 are voiced subtly to the top, establishing a line beginning with B–C–D.

The first true theme, appearing in mm. 20–22, climbs registrally and in intensity; I find that Beethoven's suggested fingering is very helpful in this tricky passage. In m. 48, the right hand effectively unites the registers of the first theme. This confluence of register prepares for the second theme, which is an astounding contrast with the first. Its pace is flexible. I play this music with as sweet and gentle a touch as possible, but tension is still inherent in this theme. I play the elements of the first theme that return in m. 58 in a triumphant manner; finally the bass plays A-flat, and the harmony is stable.

As the key of D-flat is temporarily established in mm. 98–99, the impact of C minor is temporarily lessened, and I allow the pace to slow a bit with the *espressivo* and *poco ritenente* of m. 99.

The recapitulation takes the theme to extreme registers of the piano, creating the effect of barely controlled drama.

I play the diminished chords in mm. 146–147 as strongly and emphatically as possible, changing touch with the first one in m. 148. Since the chords are all off the main beats, the rests—held for their full duration, not rushed—are crucial for maintaining the metrical frame of reference here, and thus the backbone of the music. At the end of the movement, the final chord sounds hollow, for only the upper and lower registers are played.

From the start, the **Arietta: Adagio molto semplice e cantabile** evokes feelings of spaciousness. At the beginning, I play the left hand very quietly but make sure that the general sonority is full and round. The right hand is also quiet, although it is voiced to the top to bring out the arietta line. The point at which the line opens up the most is the apex of the crescendo in m. 6, after which the intensity diminishes. I change the quality of the sound markedly for the second part of the arietta, which begins in A minor.

In this movement, Beethoven integrated variation and sonata-allegro form, and the third variation is dramatically different from the first two. Beginning *forte*, the surface motion is twice as fast again as that of its predecessor. I drop in dynamics in the right hand as the left-hand arpeggios sweep up the keyboard. Following the third variation, the musical line becomes far more abstract, but the basic harmonic and metrical backbone is unchanged. I use the left pedal throughout the *pianissimo* area and change the right pedal with every right-hand rest.

Beethoven brings back the idea of the theme with a simple reaffirmation of the three basic harmonies (C major, A minor, G major; mm. 100-105). I play these measures as two groups of three, with a substantial crescendo in each. That of the second group goes all the way to the end of the phrase. We are then faced with the issue of how to continue.

The fundamental approach of classical variation diminution has brought the music to this point but can take it no further. So after restating the three fundamental harmonies, Beethoven brought in the ultimate in diminution (or speed) -the trill.

1 Excerpted from *Playing the Beethoven Piano Sonatas* by Robert Taub
edited and abridged by Susanne Sheston

Published by Amadeus Press

The C-G-G motive is played, now *forte*, in the bass only, under the D-E trill. The trill also allows the music to dissolve, and the motive recurs in new, foreign harmonies as the trill changes to D-E-flat. At this point the music is no longer a further variation but is rather a nascent development of the generalized C-G-G motive in new harmonic contexts. The trills grow with the crescendo starting in m.114, and the bass B-flat in m.116 can be played truly sforzando, for the right-hand trill continues above it.

Development of the main thematic motive continues more explicitly in the measures that follow (mm.120-130). From m. 125 on, I keep the top line of the right hand as the main thread, while the left hand plays the light, subtle rhythmic outlines of the abstracted theme as begun in m. 120.

I elongate the last dotted eighth-note of m. 130, the only concession to the start of the recapitulation, and I keep the same tempo with which the movement began. Intensity reaches a peak in mm. 159-160, as all that is left is a trill on high G. As a near-final transformation, the theme is played with the trill in counterpoint, first above, then below. The left hand is a mere shimmer, the trills very soft, and the melodic notes not so much played as caressed.

Finally the motive C-G-G is itself inverted; it becomes G-C-C to end the sonata. This is a moment of transcendence; after nearly thirty minutes of music, time seems to stand still, even to reverse itself.

Dedicated to Archduke Rudolph

Sonata in C minor

Ludwig van Beethoven
Opus 111
Composed in 1822

a) The fingering in italics and the pedal markings are Beethoven's.

Allegro con brio ed appassionato
(♩ = 132)
cresc.
poco ritenente
mezzo piano
a tempo
cresc.
a tempo
poco ritenente
rinforz.
poco ritenente
espressivo
a tempo

b) Many editions suggest *sf* markings for the D-flat and D-natural (mm. 48–49) even though there are none in the autograph. I have chosen not to suggest them here, for this chromatic D-flat–D-natural progression is functionally different from the falling fifth C–F (mm. 114–115). The latter includes an *sf* marking, and presages the descending fifth of the coda (m. 150).

ri — tar — dan — do
adagio
tempo 1
non ligato
p cresc.
cresc.

72
p
sempre p
76
79
82
84
cresc.
86
f
sf

88
sf
sf
90
sf
92
ff
sf
p
ritar
dan
95
do
a tempo
cresc.
97
Ped.
99
espressivo
dim.
poco ritenente
a tempo
f
(sf)

c) Some editions make the C a C-flat, although there is no ♭ sign in the autograph. I believe C is correct.

d) Pedal as per autograph. e) There is no > ***p*** (as is often printed here) in the autograph. One may naturally shape the dynamics down (softer) here, but the establishment of a stable C Major is a reason to not be diminutive. f) The first edition is G–E-natural–G, not G–C–E-natural as written in the autograph.

cresc.
poi a poi sempre più allegro
8va
tempo primo
(ff)
p cresc.
ff
sf

g) Not present in the autograph. One could sustain the pedal until the first chord of the Arietta.

ARIETTA

Adagio molto semplice e cantabile (♪ = 100)

p

cresc.

sf > *p*

sf > *p*

dolce

sempre legato

p

25/26
sempre legato
28
cresc.
p
cresc.
32
1.
2.
L'istesso tempo
sf
sf
m.s.
dolce
34
sempre legato
37
cresc.

h) This tie is not present in the autograph, but does appear in the first edition.

sempre forte
sf

i) These ties are not present in both the autograph and the first edition.

61
62
64a
1.
2.
65
pp
66
sempre pp
68

70
72
leggiermente
cresc.
pp
sempre pp
74
76
78
sempre staccato
80
pp
pp

sempre pp
pp leggieremente
sempre pp

j) The E here is correct, as per both the autograph and the first edition.

104
sf
Ped.
106
f
p
dim.
pp
113
p cresc.
sf
p
p cresc.
dim.
120
espressivo
p
p
dim.
123
pp
sempre pp

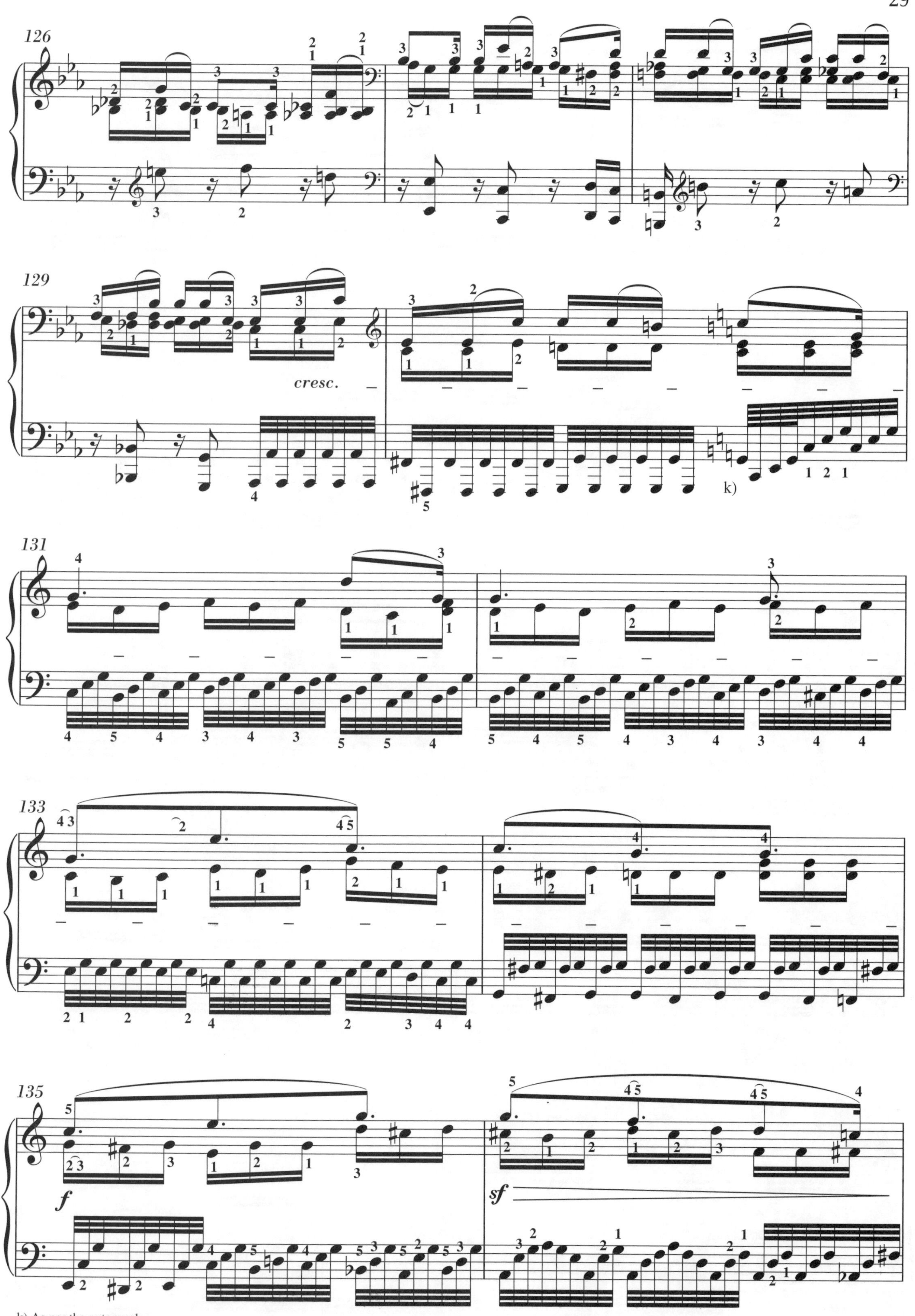

k) As per the autograph.

137
p
p
139
cresc.
141
sf
p
143
cresc.
145
sf
p
sf

147
sf
p
cresc.
149
151
153
155

157
f
159
sf
sf
sf
tr
tr
tr
sf
pp
162
164
tr
166

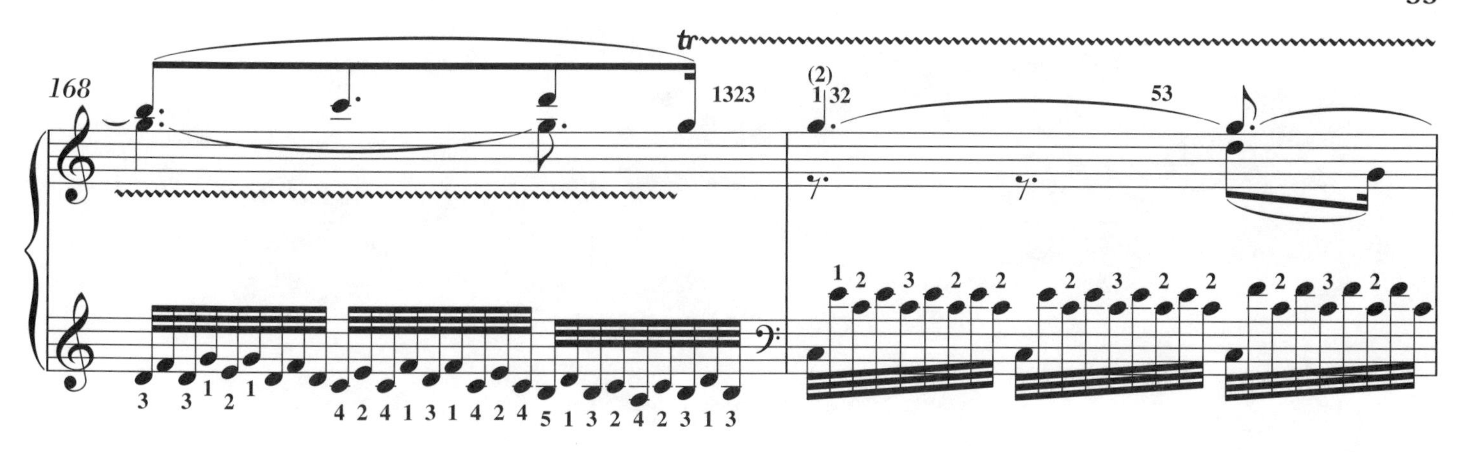
168
tr

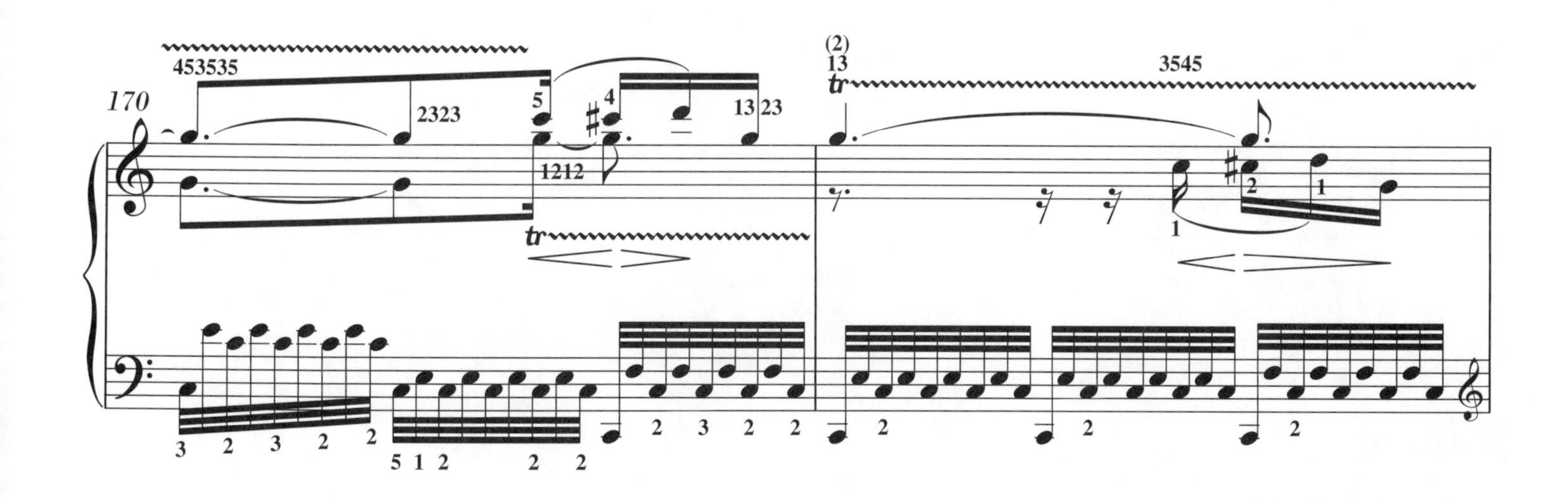
170
tr
tr

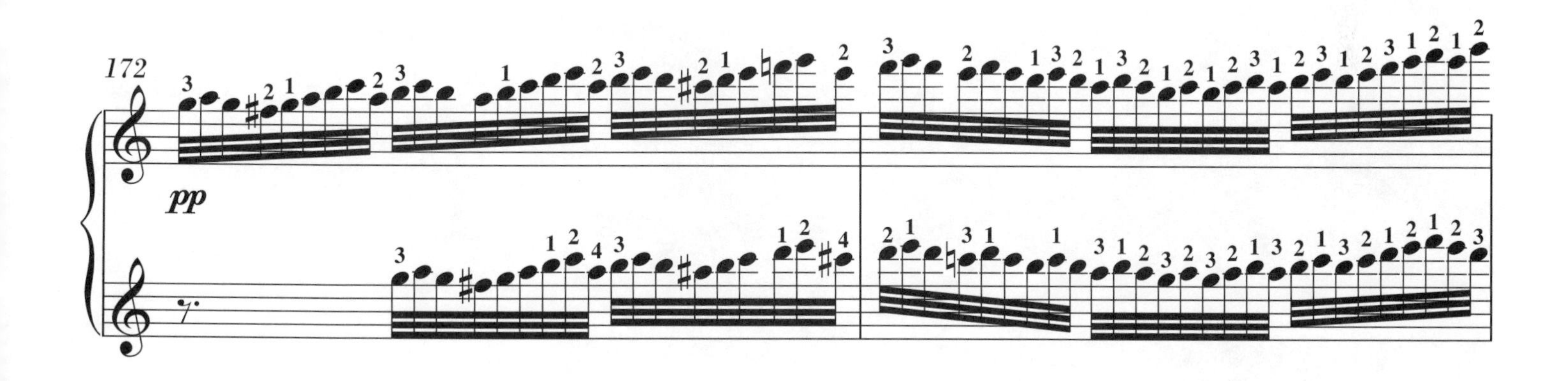
172
pp

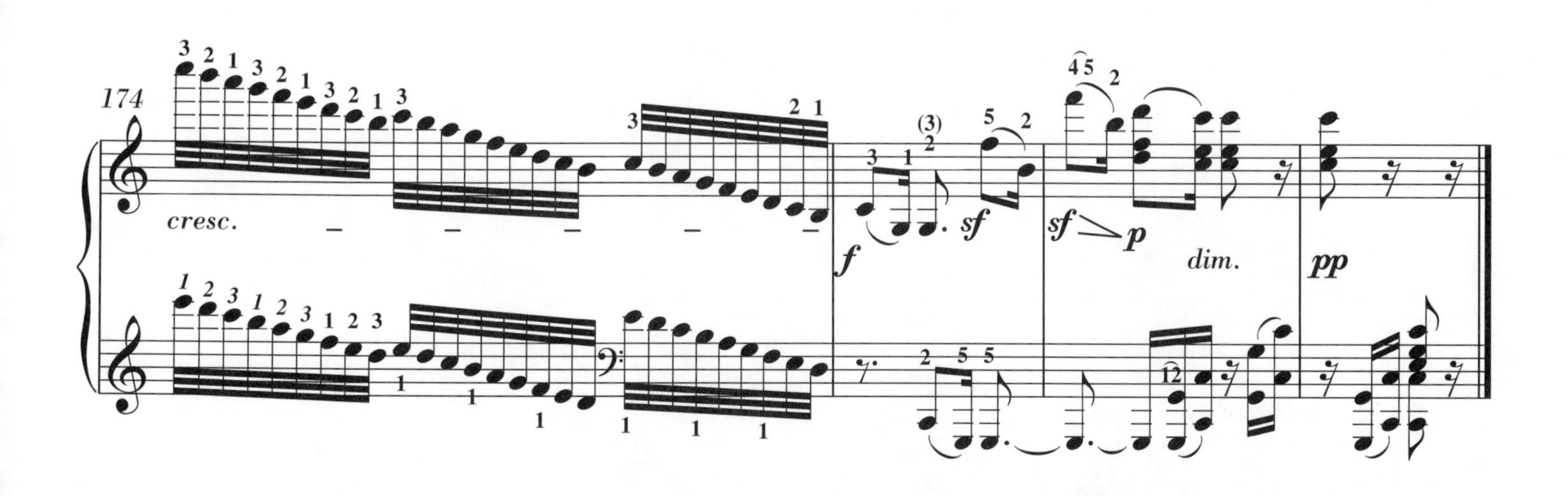
174
cresc.
f
sf
sf
p
dim.
pp

ABOUT THE EDITOR

Robert Taub

From New York's Carnegie Hall to Hong Kong's Cultural Centre to Germany's *avant garde* Zentrum für Kunst und Medientechnologie, Robert Taub is acclaimed internationally. He has performed as soloist with the MET Orchestra in Carnegie Hall, the Boston Symphony Orchestra, BBC Philharmonic, The Philadelphia Orchestra, San Francisco Symphony, Los Angeles Philharmonic, Montreal Symphony, Munich Philharmonic, Orchestra of St. Luke's, Hong Kong Philharmonic, Singapore Symphony, and others.

Robert Taub has performed solo recitals on the Great Performers Series at New York's Lincoln Center and other major series worldwide. He has been featured in international festivals, including the Saratoga Festival, the Lichfield Festival in England, San Francisco's Midsummer Mozart Festival, the Geneva International Summer Festival, among others.

Following the conclusion of his highly celebrated New York series of Beethoven Piano Sonatas, Taub completed a sold-out Beethoven cycle in London at Hampton Court Palace. His recordings of the complete Beethoven Piano Sonatas have been praised throughout the world for their insight, freshness, and emotional involvement. In addition to performing, Robert Taub is an eloquent spokesman for music, giving frequent engaging and informal lectures and pre-concert talks. His book on Beethoven—*Playing the Beethoven Piano Sonatas*—has been published internationally by Amadeus Press.

Taub was featured in a recent PBS television program—*Big Ideas*—that highlighted him playing and discussing Beethoven Piano Sonatas. Filmed during his time as Artist-in-Residence at the Institute for Advanced Study, this program has been broadcast throughout the US on PBS affiliates.

Robert Taub's performances are frequently broadcast on radio networks around the world, including the NPR (Performance Today), Ireland's RTE, and Hong Kong's RTHK. He has also recorded the Sonatas of Scriabin and works of Beethoven, Schumann, Liszt, and Babbitt for Harmonia Mundi, several of which have been selected as "critic's favorites" by *Gramophone*, *Newsweek*, *The New York Times*, *The Washington Post*, *Ovation*, and *Fanfare*.

Robert Taub is involved with contemporary music as well as the established literature, premiering piano concertos by Milton Babbitt (MET Orchestra, James Levine) and Mel Powell (Los Angeles Philharmonic), and making the first recordings of the Persichetti Piano Concerto (Philadelphia Orchestra, Charles Dutoit) and Sessions Piano Concerto. He has premiered six works of Milton Babbitt (solo piano, chamber music, Second Piano Concerto). Taub has also collaborated with several 21st-century composers, including Jonathan Dawe (USA), David Bessell (UK), and Ludger Brümmer (Germany) performing their works in America and Europe.

Taub is a Phi Beta Kappa graduate of Princeton where he was a University Scholar. As a Danforth Fellow he completed his doctoral degree at The Juilliard School where he received the highest award in piano. Taub has served as Artist-in-Residence at Harvard University, at UC Davis, as well as at the Institute for Advanced Study. He has led music forums at Oxford and Cambridge Universities and The Juilliard School. Taub has also been Visiting Professor at Princeton University and at Kingston University (UK).